Hello!
I am an
octopus.

I0115151

Can you count my arms?

Octopuses have eight arms, and each arm is covered in suckers.

My suckers help me hunt and explore.

Suckers are arranged in two rows along each arm.

Each arm of an octopus can perform tasks independently of the others.

I can multi-task.

If an octopus loses a part of an arm, it has the ability to grow it back.

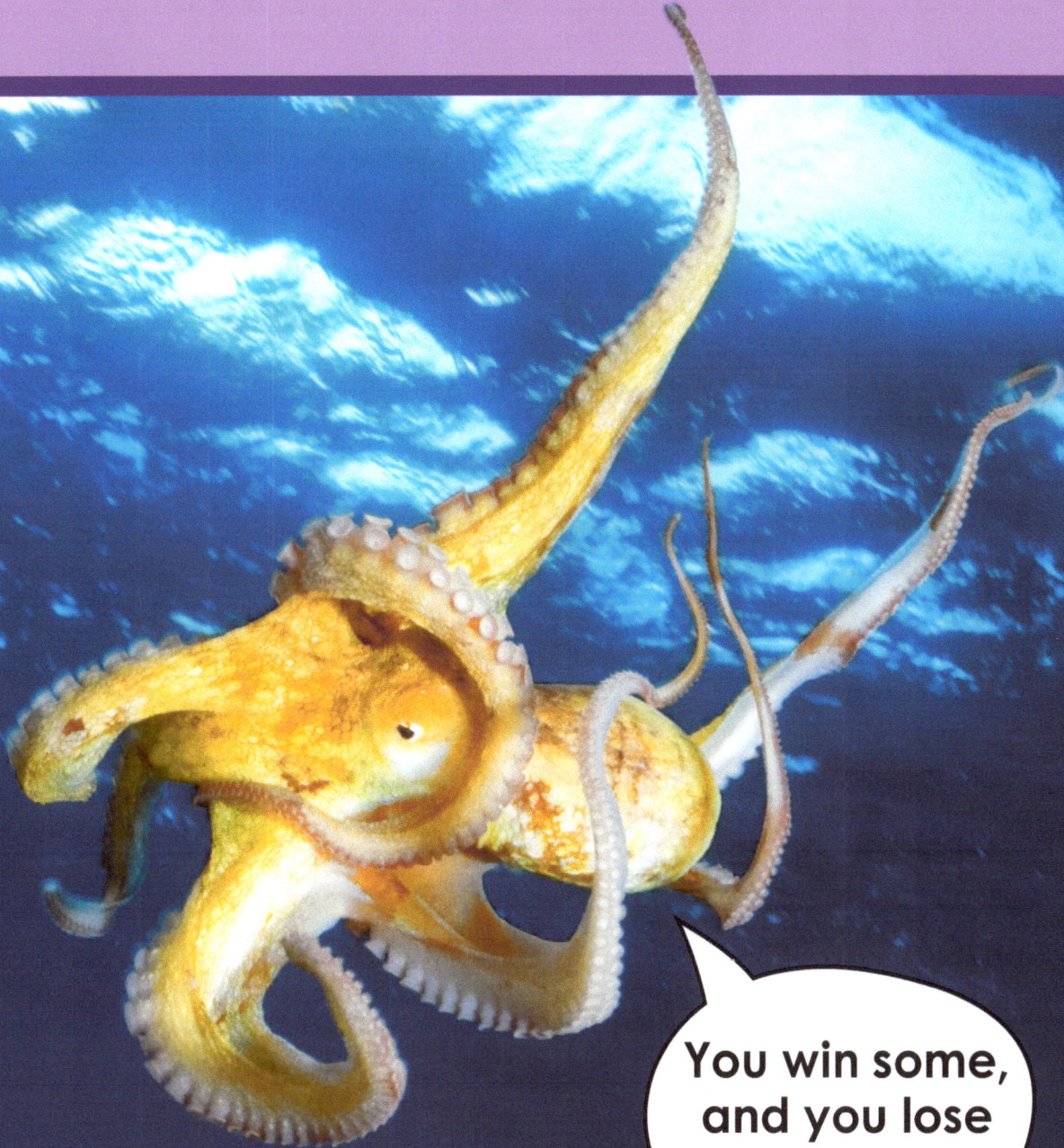

You win some, and you lose some.

Octopus suckers are highly sensitive. They can detect touch and pressure.

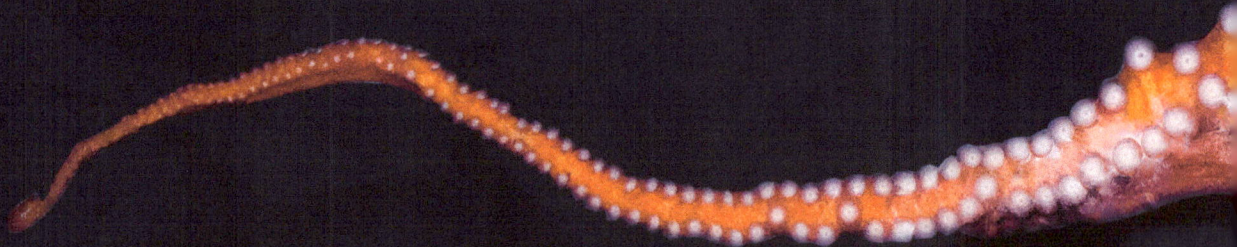

The suckers can also detect taste, temperature, and even chemicals.

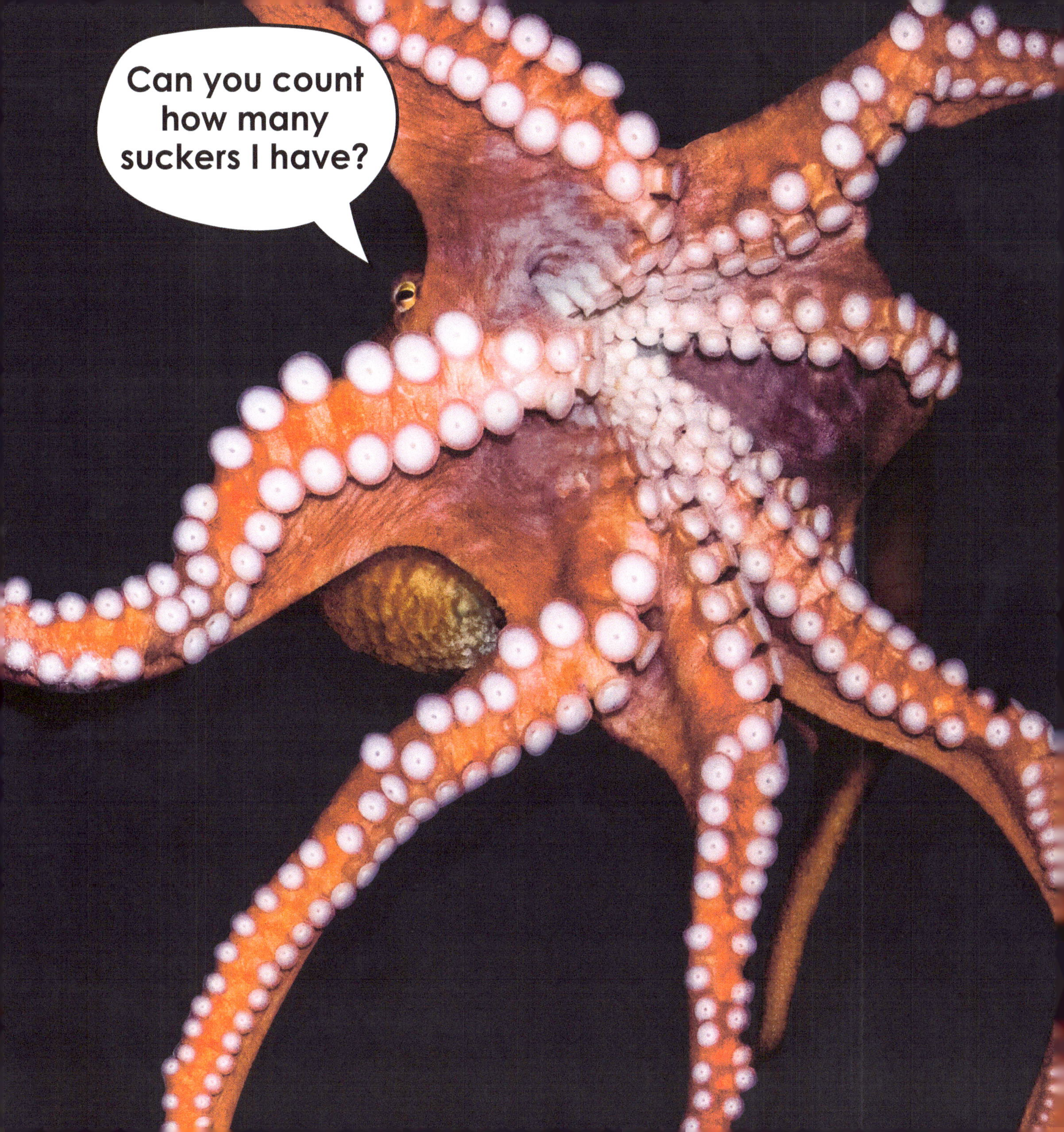
Can you count how many suckers I have?

Octopuses have a "beak" located at the base of their arms.

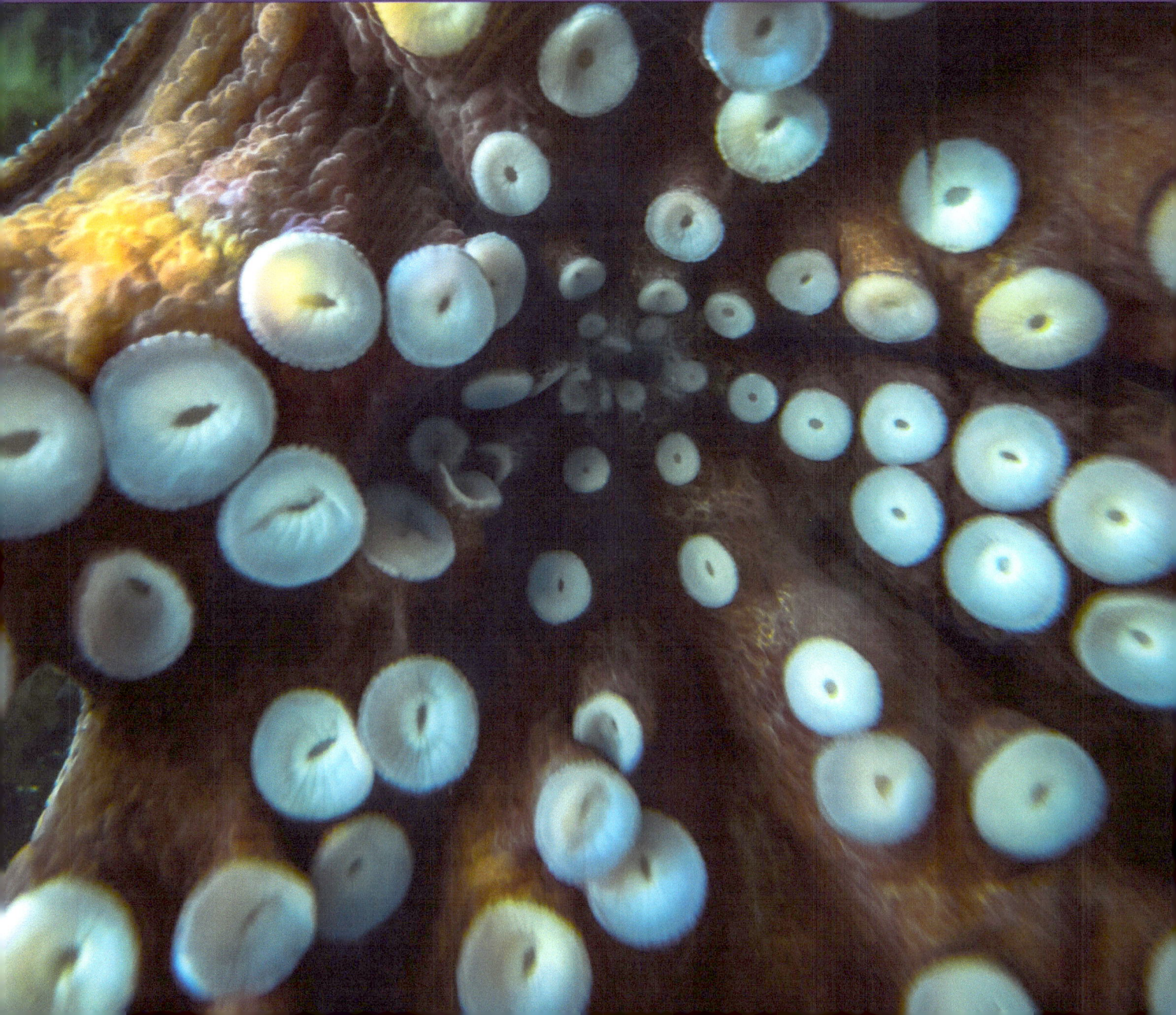

The beak works like a pair of powerful jaws.

I use my beak to crush the shells of my prey.

Octopuses have three hearts.

Two hearts pump blood to my gills.

The other pumps it to the rest of my body.

When in danger, an octopus can release a cloud of ink to create a smokescreen, allowing it to escape from predators.

The ink not only makes it hard to see, but it also has chemicals that affect a predator's sense of smell and taste.

There's no way you're catching me.

Octopuses can move quickly through the water by pushing water through a "siphon".

The siphon is tube near the octopus' head. It helps them breath under water.

Can you see my siphon? Cool, huh?

Octopuses can change the color and texture of their skin to blend in with their surroundings.

Shhh. I'm hiding from predators.

Octopuses use color changes to communicate with each other.

Octopus bodies are soft and flexible.

I don't have any bones in my body.

Octopuses can adjust their body posture to copy specific objects.

Nothing to see here. Just another bunch of coral.

They can fit just about anywhere.

Octopuses are usually solitary animals and prefer to live alone.

Most octopuses have a short lifespan, ranging from 6 months to a few years.

Female octopuses lay thousands of eggs in one go.

I'll protect them until they hatch.

Octopus babies grow quickly. They can swim and hunt right after hatching.

I'd better get to work.

Octopuses have highly developed eyes and excellent vision.

I can see well at night too.

Octopuses hunt at night.

Octopuses are very intelligent and are known for their problem-solving skills.

I can figure it out.

Octopuses are curious about their environment and can learn from others around them.

Ohhh. I get it now.

Some octopus species are able to live in the deep sea.

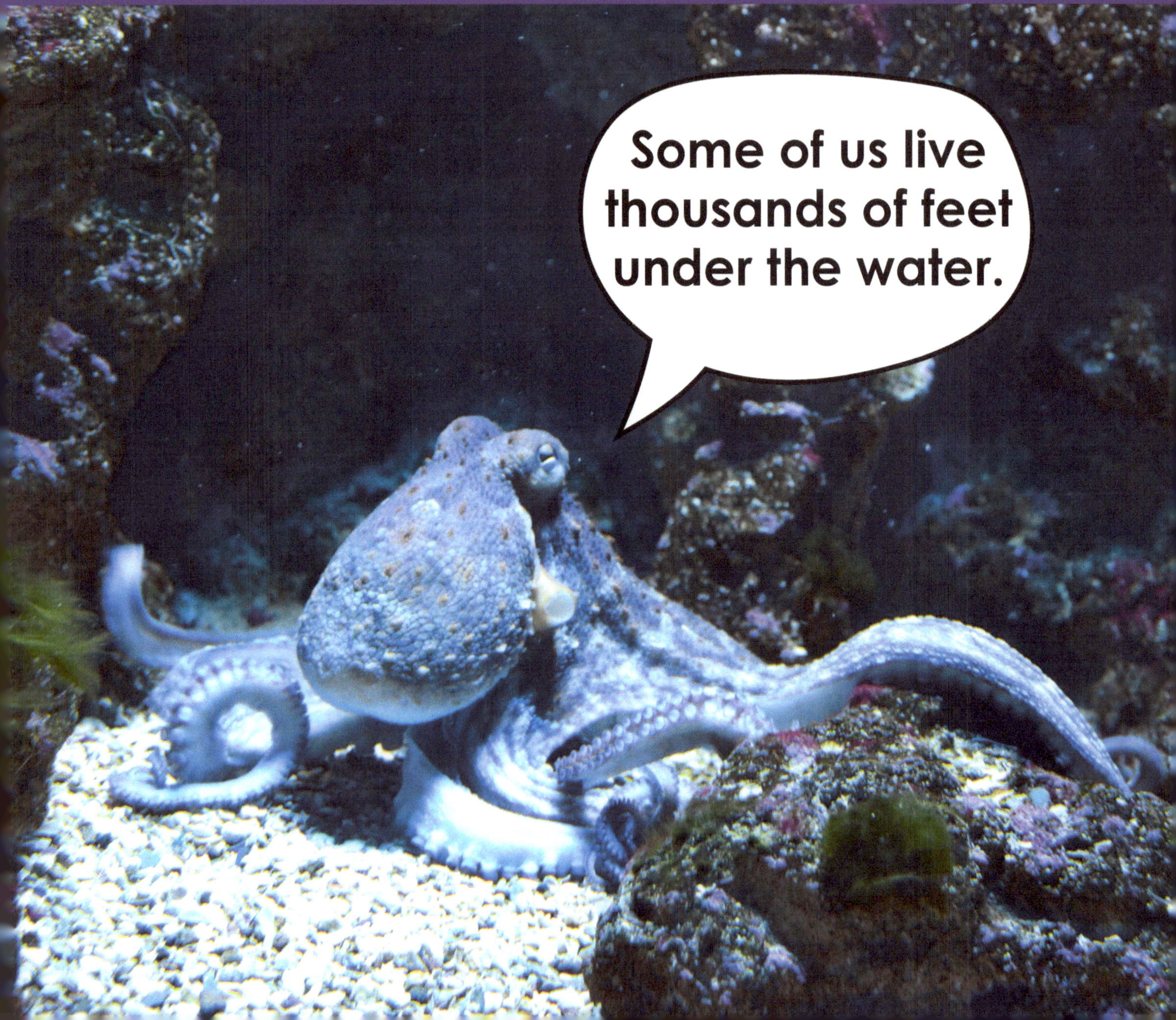

Octopuses also live in shallow water and costal areas.

Want more?

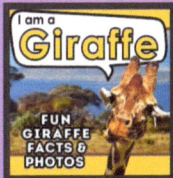      

  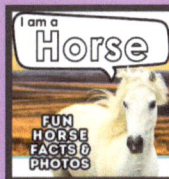    

     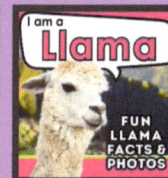 

  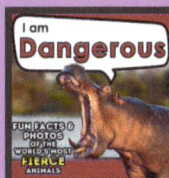     ... and more

COLLECT THEM ALL!

ActiveBrainsBooks.com

Hello parents!

scan here

Visit us to find out about new releases and *FREE* offers. We'll let you know when we have a new release coming out and how you can get it for FREE.
And you can cast your vote for what book we make next!

ActiveBrainsBooks.com

or visit here

---

scan here

Let us know what you think. As an independent publisher, your honest reviews mean a lot to us and our business. We'd love to hear from you!

amazon.com/review/create-review/

or visit here

FOLLOW US on Amazon.

amazon.com/author/activebrainsbooks

ActiveBrainsBooks.com

ACTIVE
BRAINS

www.ingramcontent.com/pod-product-compliance
Lightning Source LLC
Chambersburg PA
CBHW060845270326
41933CB00003B/198